Grandma's Dead

Breaking Bad News with Baby Animals

BOXTREE

Amanda McCall *and* **Ben Schwartz**

First published 2008 by Boxtree
an imprint of Pan Macmillan Ltd
Pan Macmillan, 20 New Wharf Road, London N1 9RR
Basingstoke and Oxford
Associated companies throughout the world
www.panmacmillan.com

ISBN 978-0-7522-2683-5

A CIP catalogue record for this book is available from
the British Library.

Printed by Printer Trento, Italy

Visit **www.panmacmillan.com** to read more about all our books
and to buy them. You will also find features, author interviews and
news of any author events, and you can sign up for e-newsletters
so that you're always first to hear about our new releases.

Introduction

Afraid to tell your girlfriend her bum looks big in that? Need to let your neighbours know you're a registered sex offender? Why not let a lovable baby bunny in a basket do it for you?

Grandma's Dead: Breaking Bad News with Baby Animals softens the blow of even the harshest news, saving you anxiety and time. In this day and age, who has the time to spend a long, tearful afternoon explaining to young Bobby that his daddy's never coming home? Especially when there are three happy puppies in a pumpkin patch eager to do it for you!

Even better, sending a baby animal postcard provides the recipient with a precious keepsake that can be cherished for years to come. This way, you'll never have to remind your wife that you cheated on her—she can treasure that memory on a postcard forever!

No matter how sensitive the subject or awkward the circumstance, *Grandma's Dead: Breaking Bad News with Baby Animals* provides an adorable solution to life's stickiest situations!

Breaking Bad News
with Baby Animals

You don't matter

Breaking Bad News
with Baby Animals

_____

_____

_____

Breaking Bad News
with Baby Animals

_____

_____

_____

Breaking Bad News
with Baby Animals

Breaking Bad News
with Baby Animals

The donor backed out

Breaking Bad News
with Baby Animals

_____

_____

_____

Breaking Bad News
with Baby Animals

Breaking Bad News
with Baby Animals

_____

_____

_____

Breaking Bad News
with Baby Animals

_____

_____

_____

Breaking Bad News
with Baby Animals

_____

_____

_____

Breaking Bad News
with Baby Animals

_____

_____

_____

Breaking Bad News
with Baby Animals

Breaking Bad News
with Baby Animals

_____

_____

_____

Your toupée isn't fooling anyone

Breaking Bad News
with Baby Animals

_____

_____

_____

Breaking Bad News
with Baby Animals

Breaking Bad News
with Baby Animals

_____

_____

_____

Breaking Bad News
with Baby Animals

_____

_____

_____

You're the father

Breaking Bad News
with Baby Animals

Breaking Bad News
with Baby Animals

Breaking Bad News
with Baby Animals

Breaking Bad News
with Baby Animals

_____

_____

_____

Breaking Bad News
with Baby Animals

It's only sunny because there's a hole in the ozone layer

Breaking Bad News
with Baby Animals

_____

_____

_____

Breaking Bad News
with Baby Animals

Grandpa left you nothing

Breaking Bad News
with Baby Animals

Breaking Bad News
with Baby Animals

Breaking Bad News
with Baby Animals

_____

_____

_____

Breaking Bad News
with Baby Animals

Breaking Bad News
with Baby Animals

Mum found your stash

Breaking Bad News
with Baby Animals

Yes, your bum looks fat in that

Breaking Bad News
with Baby Animals

_____

_____

_____

Breaking Bad News
with Baby Animals

Breaking Bad News
with Baby Animals

_____

_____

_____

Recycling won't help

Breaking Bad News
with Baby Animals

_____

_____

_____

Breaking Bad News
with Baby Animals

_____

_____

_____

I'm saving myself for marriage

Breaking Bad News
with Baby Animals

_____

_____

_____

Breaking Bad News
with Baby Animals

Breaking Bad News
with Baby Animals

_____

_____

_____

Breaking Bad News
with Baby Animals

_____

_____

_____

Breaking Bad News
with Baby Animals

_____

_____

_____

Acknowledgments

We would like to thank Jud Laghi, Rachel Miller, Jesse Hara, Stephanie Meyers, Bruce Nichols, Laura Dozier, Liz Kaye, Sharon Eide, Elizabeth Flynn, Tom Vezo, Adam Jones, Steve Dressler, and our loving families, who taught us everything we know about avoiding confrontation.

_____

Photo Credits

About the Authors

AMANDA MCCALL is the author of *Hold My Gold: A White Girl's Guide to the Hip-Hop World* and *Britney's Baby Book*. Her work has been featured in numerous publications including the *New York Times*, *Vanity Fair*, the *Los Angeles Times*, *Allure*, *New York* magazine, *Los Angeles* magazine, *Vibe*, and Gawker.com. She has appeared on the *Late Show with David Letterman*, E! Entertainment Television, ABC News Now, New York City's CW11, and a variety of American radio shows.

BEN SCHWARTZ is a writer/actor/comedian from New York City. He was a staff writer on the third season of Adult Swim's Emmy-nominated show *Robot Chicken*, as well as a freelance writer for *Saturday Night Live*'s Weekend Update and the *Late Show with David Letterman*'s monologue. Although many of his jokes made it to air, Ben created a website to give his rejected jokes and short films a home—RejectedJokes.com. Along with acting in television shows and feature films, Ben is a sketch and improv comedian at the Upright Citizens Brigade Theatre and has performed in shows around the world, including the Montreal Just for Laughs Comedy Festival.